W9-CGN-076

The 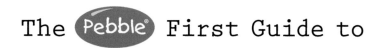 First Guide to

Rocks and Minerals

by Zachary Pitts

Consulting Editor: Gail Saunders-Smith, PhD

Consultant: Steven Losh, PhD
Department of Chemistry and Geology
Minnesota State University, Mankato

Capstone
press®

Mankato, Minnesota

Pebble Books are published by Capstone Press,
151 Good Counsel Drive, P.O. Box 669, Mankato, Minnesota 56002.
www.capstonepress.com

1 2 3 4 5 6 13 12 11 10 09 08

Library of Congress Cataloging-in-Publication Data
Pitts, Zachary.
    The Pebble first guide to rocks and minerals / by Zachary Pitts.
    p. cm. — (Pebble Books. Pebble first guides)
    Includes bibliographical references and index.
    ISBN-13: 978-1-4296-1711-6 (hardcover)
    ISBN-10: 1-4296-1711-X (hardcover)
    ISBN-13: 978-1-4296-2805-1 (softcover pbk.)
    ISBN-10: 1-4296-2805-7 (softcover pbk.)
    1. Rocks — Juvenile literature. 2. Minerals — Juvenile literature. I. Title. II. Series.
QE432.2.P58 2009
552 — dc22   2008001399

Summary: A basic field guide format introduces 13 rocks and minerals.

About Rocks and Minerals

Minerals are solid materials made by nature. Rocks are
also made by nature, but a rock is made of more than one
mineral. This book features both rocks and minerals.

Note to Parents and Teachers

The Pebble First Guides set supports science standards related
to life science. In a reference format, this book describes and
illustrates 13 rocks and minerals. This book introduces early readers
to subject-specific vocabulary words, which are defined in the
Glossary section. Early readers may need assistance to read some
words and to use the Table of Contents, Glossary, Read More,
Internet Sites, and Index sections of the book.

Table of Contents

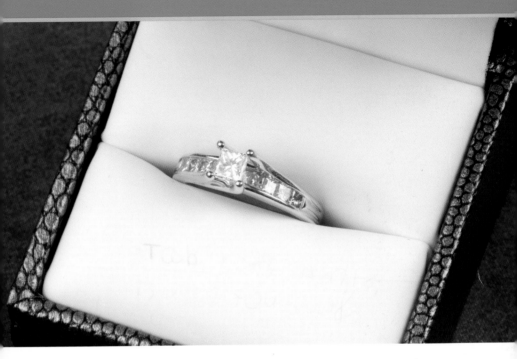

What It Looks Like:

    most are colorless crystals

Where It's Found:

    Brazil, India, South Africa

Facts: • world's hardest mineral

       • used for jewelry

What It Looks Like:
black or gray, metallic

Where It's Found:
China, Brazil, Canada, Madagascar, Sri Lanka

Facts:
- used in pencils
- feels greasy

What It Looks Like:

colorless crystal cubes

Where It's Found:

England, Germany, Poland, United States

Facts:
- can be taken out of sea water or mined
- used to melt ice

9

What It Looks Like:

black, metallic

Where It's Found:

South Africa, Sweden, United States

Facts:
- can be made into magnets
- has iron in it

11

What It Looks Like:

black, brown, green, violet,
or colorless; shiny

Where It's Found:

Brazil, India, Madagascar, United States

Facts: • breaks into smooth, thin sheets
• used in paints

What It Looks Like:

golden-yellow; shiny cubes

Where It's Found:

Japan, Spain, United States

Facts:
- sometimes called "fool's gold" because it looks like gold
- used in some types of jewelry

What It Looks Like:
glassy; colorless, white, gray, purple, pink or other colors

Where It's Found:
China, Japan, Russia, United States

Facts:
- amethyst is a type of quartz
- used in watches and radios

amethyst

What It Looks Like:

black, shiny

Where It's Found:

Australia, China, United States

Facts:
- a type of coal
- made of plants that lived millions of years ago

What It Looks Like:
pink and white

Where It's Found:
India, Italy, United States

Facts:
- used in buildings
- Mount Rushmore in South Dakota is granite

20

What It Looks Like:

white, gray, or black; may have fossils

Where It's Found:

Belgium, China, England, Egypt,
United States

Facts:
- Pyramids of Egypt are limestone
- chalk is a type of limestone

What It Looks Like:

red, white, yellow, green

Where It's Found:

Canada, Italy, Greece, Spain, United States

Facts:
- used to make sculptures
- lots of heat and pressure turn limestone into marble

Lincoln Memorial

What It Looks Like:

grayish-white; full of small holes

Where It's Found:

near volcanoes in Chile, Greece, Italy, United States

Facts:
- used in some soaps
- floats in water

27

What It Looks Like:

    light gray, red, brown, or green

Where It's Found:

    Brazil, China, India, United States

Facts: • used to make buildings

        • made of sand that is mostly quartz

Glossary

crystal — a solid substance having a regular pattern of many flat surfaces

fossil — the remains or traces of something that once lived

greasy — shiny and wet with an oily substance

iron — a very hard metal

metallic — looks like metal and can be dull or bright

mine — to dig up minerals that are underground

mineral — a solid found in nature that is not made by people, animals, or plants; minerals can be found on earth's surface or underground.

rock — a collection of minerals stuck together by heat or pressure over time

sculpture — something carved or shaped out of rock

Read More

Dayton, Connor. *Minerals*. Rocks and Minerals. New York: PowerKids Press, 2007.

Mattern, Joanne. *Minerals and the Rock Cycle*. Shaping and Reshaping of Earth's Surface. New York: PowerKids Press, 2006.

Internet Sites

FactHound offers a safe, fun way to find Internet sites related to this book. All of the sites on FactHound have been researched by our staff.

Here's how:

1. Visit *www.facthound.com*
2. Choose your grade level.
3. Type in this book ID **142961711X** for age-appropriate sites. You may also browse subjects by clicking on letters, or by clicking on pictures and words.
4. Click on the **Fetch It** button.

FactHound will fetch the best sites for you!

Index

Grade: 1
Early-Intervention Level: 26

Editorial Credits
Erika L. Shores, editor; Alison Thiele, designer; Jo Miller, photo researcher;
Sarah L. Schuette, photo stylist; Marcy Morin, scheduler

Photo Credits
Alamy/Eric Nathan, 4; Philip Scalia, 19
Capstone Press/Karon Dubke, cover (all), 5, 6, 7, 10, 11, 12 (both), 13, 14, 16,
17 (top), 18, 20, 22 (both), 24 (both), 26, 27, 28
Getty Images Inc./DEA/A. Rizzi, 17 (bottom); DEA/C. Bevilaqua, 8;
Spencer Platt, 9; Stone/Glen Allison, 29
Shutterstock/Cristina Ciochina, 25; Jonathan Larsen, 21; sculpies, 23
SuperStock Inc./age footstock, 15

The Capstone Press Photo Studio thanks Bryce Hoppie and Minnesota State University,
Mankato for providing the rock and mineral samples that appear in this book.